N.M. SURTEES

IDEA GENERATION

**The Ultimate Guide to Inspirational Ideas That Would Motivate
You to Action, Discover the Empowered Thoughts and Wisdom of
the Century That Would Absolutely Inspire You**

Descrierea CIP a Bibliotecii Naționale a României
N.M. SURTEES
   IDEA GENERATION. The Ultimate Guide to Inspirational Ideas That Would Motivate You to Action, Discover the Empowered Thoughts and Wisdom of the Century That Would Absolutely Inspire You / N.M. Surtees. – Bucharest: Editura My Ebook, 2020
   ISBN 978-606-983-586-9

N.M. SURTEES

IDEA GENERATION

The Ultimate Guide to Inspirational Ideas That Would Motivate You to Action, Discover the Empowered Thoughts and Wisdom of the Century That Would Absolutely Inspire You

My Ebook Publishing House
Bucharest, 2020

TABLE OF CONTENTS

FOREWORD

Inspirational ideas *"Get inspired and Empowered with the most inspiring thoughts and wisdom of the century"* is an eBook that aims at enlightening readers on how they can live inspired lives. There are so many people who live their whole lives without ever realizing their full potentials. All that these people needed was simply some inspiration to empower them.

In this eBook, you will get to learn what empowerment means. You will also get to learn the different definitions of the word "inspired". You will also learn in detail what an inspired idea means. This introduction prepares your mind to more insights that you will get in the course of reading the book. By the final chapter you will be able to clearly understand what it means to be inspired and empowered.

There are so many types of inspirational ideas that can empower individuals. This book takes a look at some of these ideas. As a reader, you will be able to establish which category you fall in. There is also a group of ideas that normally apply for everybody. All this will be discussed in the eBook.

Many people wonder where inspirational thoughts come from. Well reading this book, will provide you with some valuable inspirations that can help you make significant changes in your life. You will also get to find out other places where you can find these ideas. You will learn how other people managed to get good inspirational ideas that shaped their life's successes.

Getting empowered is normally a process. It doesn't really just occur overnight. In this eBook, you will learn more about this process. This can help you in your own empowerment. It can also help you in empowering other people. You will also learn the main challenges faced during the empowerment of a group of people or an individual. All this will prepare you for the process.

Many people have so many good inspirational thoughts. They meet people who impact on them positively. They also get ideas that could possibly change their lives. Sadly, most of these people end up not using their ideas at all. They practically have the key to success but end up losing it or storing it away. In this eBook, you will learn how not to fall into this category of people. You will learn how to use inspirational thoughts and ideas to empower yourself.

There is nothing as bad as going through life with no inspiration. You will lack the motivation to pursue your dreams. You may also end up living an unfulfilling life. In this eBook, you will learn factors that make people loose inspiration. You will also get tips on how to avoid this. Many people are living sad lives without knowing that they have the ability to change this. Readers of this book will learn how to not to be one of these people. They will learn how to change their minds and other factors so as to achieve success in life.

An inspired person is a very powerful person. This is a person who possesses the full capability of changing the world and not just their personal lives. In this eBook, you will learn about famous people who managed to use their thoughts to change History. They also managed to empower multitudes of other people. Learn more about this people. You will be inspired in the process.

This eBook doesn't only aim at empowering you. It also teaches you how you can be an inspiration to other people. By helping others, you will also be more inspired. In addition, you can live a fulfilling life knowing they you played a key role in helping others achieve their dreams.

Many people fail to achieve their dreams simply through lack of trying. Fear is an enemy to success. Learning and educating yourself is one way to ensure that you don't let life pass you by. Another reason why many people fail is due to negative thinking. There is power in having a positive attitude. This can help you make the most out of your dreams and aim to achieve what others may term as "the impossible".

"Nothing can stop a man with the right mental attitude from achieving his goal; nothing on earth can help the man with the wrong mental attitude".

Thomas Jefferson

This eBook is written in simple English. The examples given are applicable to everyday life situations. The famous people discussed in some chapters are popular people whose lives many can relate to. This makes it very easy to understand it and to implement the ideas shared.

Inspirational Ideas

Get Inspired And Empowered With The Most Inspiring Thoughts And Wisdom Of The Century

CHAPTER 1

AN OVERVIEW OF THE INSPIRATIONAL IDEAS AND EMPOWERMENT

Synopsis

"To live is the rarest thing on earth. Most people exist and that's it"

Oscar Wilde

Inspirational ideas are meant to get people inspired. In this chapter, we look at what it means to be inspired and also empowered.

➤ Who are inspired people?

➤ What are the empowered?

Inspiration can change people's lives. It can help a person to start living and realize their full potential in life.

The Basics

What Does It Mean To Be Inspired?

There a number of definitions for the word "inspiration", some of these include,

- *"A divine influence directly exerted on the mind or soul" Excerpt from www.definitions.net*

- *"To get excited about life and to learn how to live" .Anonymous*

- *"To get passionate about something". Anonymous*
- *"To be inspired by something or someone is to take in a new idea and literally let it change your life". Anonymous*

Inspiration is also best defined as, arousing the mind to unusual creativity and awakening the soul of a person to enable them to pursue this creativity.

Inspiration is very important. It can help a person learn how to live more positively. It impacts on the brain of an individual and has the capability of changing their whole mindset.

For example," *The future belongs to those who believe in the beauty of their dreams."* Eleanor Roosevelt. This is a very simple yet very powerful inspirational quote. It can inspire someone who had given up on their dreams to start believing again. This can get them in to start pursuing the dream again. It also inspires people who may be pursuing their dreams but feel like they are far from achieving it. This encourages them to keep dreaming and believing.

The power of inspiration can never be underestimated. It can practically save a person's life. Someone who may have given up on life and even contemplating suicide may suddenly turn around and start living their lives to the fullest.

The right kind of inspiration can enabled you to do anything you want. You can write, an artist be a poet, a successful businessman, design and so much more. Being inspired will enable you to live a happy and more fulfilling life.

Inspirational Ideas

"Keep your face to the sunshine and you will never see the shadow"

Helen Keller

Inspirational ideas normally contain an inspiration message meant to empower individuals. There are so many types of such ideas. There are some that touch different professionals while others are meant for everyone.

An inspirational idea may just be what a person needs to get started on their careers. For instance, people who rely on creativity tend to get moments when they feel like they have run out ideas. The right of inspiration can get such a person back on track. It can also enable them to go beyond their expectations.

Inspirational ideas may also empower people to try out new opportunities and fully utilize their potentials.

Empowerment

Empowerment can be spiritual, social, political or even economic. It basically refers to strengthening a person or a group of people. This enables them to be more confident and learn to live their lives to the fullest.

There are people who may be oppressed or marginalized due to man factors. One such factor may be the society. For instance, in some societies women are normally marginalized. In this case, to empower them would be to give them confidence and opportunity to overcome all barriers and excel in different fields and learn how to be self-sufficient. It may also mean to simply enable them to enjoy opportunities that others have been enjoying but they have not. For example, the rights to be employed or even drive.

Empowerment can also be effected in organizations whereby employees are normally limited by the management. To empower them would mean to give them some kind of independence to make their own decisions and trust their own judgment. This may help in improving the working environment and overall performance of the employees.

In other instance, people may actually inhibit themselves. Negative thoughts can easily make a person doubt themselves and put themselves down. This attitude would greatly hinder their performance and their whole outlook on life.

CHAPTER 2

AN OVERVIEW OF THE TYPES
OF INSPIRATIONAL IDEAS

Synopsis

There are general inspirational ideas that can inspire any group of individuals while there are others that are meant for a group of people. In this chapter, we look at the different types of inspirational ideas.

➢ Which inspirational ideas can apply to your current situation?

➢ How can these ideas help you?

There are other ideas that may be intended for a group of people but can also be applied by other different groups.

An Overview

Visionaries

> *"When one door of happiness closes, another opens but often we look so long at the closed door that we don't see the one that has been opened for us".*
>
> *Helen Keller*

Inspirational ideas that fall under this category are meant to enable people to have a positive outlook on life. They encourage and motivate at the same time. They give people hope for the future.

Visionaries shave a clear picture of the future. They have goals and dreams. This is what keeps them motivated and enables them to pursue these goals. Having a vision also helps one in overcoming obstacle since they have their eyes set on the goals. A person who has a vision will be able to avoid things that may distract from their goals.

"Nothing splendid was ever achieved except by those who dared to believe that something inside them was superior to their circumstances".

Bruce Barton

As indicated in this inspirational idea, a visionary can easily overcome their preset circumstance. For example, a person may be poor but they have a clear vision of what they to be in future. This will give them the determination to overcome their present situation and achieve their goals. In contrast, someone who isn't inspired will just accept their present situation and be content.

Visionaries Who Have Used Inspired Ideas to Change History

There are a number of great people who managed to achieve the impossible simply by being inspired and having a vision. One such person is Nelson Mandela. This man had an idea of what he wanted South Africa to be. He had a dream of the country being free from apartheid and South Africans being able to leave in freedom.

This vision and dreams got him imprisoned for over 25 years. However, he still didn't lose sight of his vision. This is what got him released and later elected as the president of independent South Africa. After years of racism and apartheid and indescribable human suffering, South Africa is not only free but the most developed nation in the whole continent. All this was because of an inspired idea that one man had. It managed to empower him and a whole nation.

The Wright brothers are also visionaries who were inspired to create and ended up changing the course of History forever. These brothers are accredited with having invented airplanes. The two had an idea of air transportation long before anyone had even such an idea. This was way back in 1903. They made a few futile attempts but didn't give up until they have a breakthrough. This goes to show the power of a single inspirational idea.

The current president (44th) of the United States of America, Barrack Obama is another visionary. This was the first time that America elected a black man. For a country that has battle with issues of racism for hundreds of years, this was a very great milestone. If you look at the history of racism in America; it is hard to believe that the national is now being led by a black man. In historic times, this was a country that strongly supported enslaving of back people, lynching and also other racial disintegration practices, nobody that this would ever be possible. Barrack Obama not only empowered black people in United States but also inspired people from all over the world.

President Barrack Obama not only managed to inspire and empower Black people in America. He has managed to inspired people from all walks of life all over the world.

There are many people who have managed to use inspired ideas to empower themselves and the others. Their ideas and dreams have influenced the course of History. This goes to show that anyone with can go very fair in life by just being inspired.

> *"Never tell me that the sky is the limit when there are footprints on the moon"*
>
> *Author unknown*

An inspired idea can help you take a leap and step away from your current situation no matter how limiting.

Poetry

> *'To see the world is a world in a grain of sand, And heaven in a world of flower,*
> *Hold infinity in the palm of your hand, And eternity in an hour."*
>
> *William Blake*

This is another category of inspirational ideas. They serve two main purposes, the inspire poets and can also be inspiration by poets.

Inspirational ideas that are meant to inspire poets are normally helpful especially for those who have run out ideas on what to write about. They may be inspirational in that they provide ideas for topics. They may also provide tips on how to get over the mental block and become creative again.

The inspirational poems that are meant to inspire others are thought provoking. They contain a message that may be immediately clearly while others may depend on the individual interpretation of the message. For example:

"This is my quest to follow that star,
No matter how hopeless, no matter how far,
To fight for the right without question or pause,
to be willing to match into Heaven for a Heavenly cause".

Jim Darion

Such inspirational words inspire people to follow their dreams no matter what happens.

Artists

"Every child is an artist; the problem is who to remain an artist once he grows up"

Picasso

There are so many inspirational ideas that you can get from artists. In most cases, the inspirational ideas are meant for other artists. However, an individual can try and apply the same ideas to their own personal life even if they aren't artists.

For example:

> *"You can dream, create, design and build the most wonderful place in the world, but it requires people to make the dream a reality"*
>
> *Walt Disney*

This isn't just inspiration for artists; it can apply to any person. It acts a reminder that we do need people in our lives. No matter how successful you become, you will need people.

> *"I don't know the key to success, but they key failure is to try and please everybody"*
>
> *Bill Cosby*

There are also a number of inspirational ideas that are meant to inspire artists to get motivation for their works. For instance, you can get ideas for the bets locations for your art projects. Some of these ideas include Art classes, Art fairs, museums and also reading books. Some ideas recommend talking to children to get new ideas for Art. Others suggest the change of a medium.

Writers

There are so many nice inspirational ideas that are meant to inspire writers. These ideas can offer assistance to writers who are struggling or have a "writer's block". They can also be helpful to writers who are looking for inspiration to finally start writing. Most of these ideas are from successful writers.

Some of the inspirational ideas for writers include, reading the novel or writing by one of your favorite writers. This may act as an inspiration to you. Another idea is to give yourself a treat every day that you manage to accomplish a writing goal. This will keep you motivated. It is also good to be confident and persistent.

Any writer who feels stumped can get empowered to write again by just finding the right inspirational ideas.

There are also a number of inspirational ideas from writers to everyone else. These are not necessarily just meant for other writers.

- "Do not look back in anger, or forward in fear but around in awareness". James Thurber

- "The best way to cheer yourself up is to cheer someone else up". Mark Twain

- "Passionate people embrace what they love and never give up". Danielle Kennedy

All these are inspirations by writers.

Leadership

> *"The ultimate measure of a man is not where he stands in moments of comforts and convenience but where he stands in moments of challenge and controversy. The true neighbor will risk his position, his prestige and even his life for the welfare of others"*
>
> *Martin Luther King Jr*

There are so many inspirational ideas that can empower one into a leadership role. These ideas can also inspire leaders into embracing their roles and being even better leaders. The inspirational ideas are also foe leaders to use to inspire others. Some of these ideas include:

A good leader should be passionate about the goals and objectives of the team that he is leading. This is what will inspire others to work hard. A leader who lacks passion will not inspire his people. A good leader should be a good listener. His people should feel empowered to make contributions and share their ideas about the team. Another great idea is to make the members of the team feel included and appreciated. It's not possible to inspire them if at all they feel left out in the key role such as decision making.

> *"Leaders arrant born, they are made. And they are made just like anything else, through hard work. And that's the price that we'll have to pay to achieve the goal or any other goal"*
>
> *Vince Lombardi*

Business Inspirational Ideas

There are so many different types of inspirational ideas for business people. The first type is the kind of inspiration that is normally given to people who want to get started in business. These maybe people who are passionate about a business ideas but they lack the confidence to pursue this. They may be hindered by fear or failure of self-doubt. These inspirational ideas empower such people to go ahead and start their own business. It prepares them for the challenges of running a business. The right kind of ideas not only helps a business person to get started out but to keep going no matter what they encounter.

There are also inspirational ideas for people who are currently facing hardships in their businesses. Maybe they have been hit by financial crisis or the business is just not doing as well as expected. Inspirational ideas can help such business people to remain hopeful in trying to get over their hurdles. They may be inspired into looking for alternative financiers. They may also be inspired to try out new ideas that may just give the business the right kind of boost. If the business completely failed, inspirational ideas would give the businessman the confidence to move on and try out something new.

There are also inspirational ideas on how to empower employees of any organizations. The right kind of empowerment can get the staff members motivated and enable them to perform much better. Some of the inspirational ideas include, including the employees in the decision making process, listening to them and also incorporating their ideas as suggested. In some organizations, there are inspirational quotes shared around to keep the employees motivated at all times.

Religious Inspiration

There are a lot of different types of inspirational ideas that are provided by different religious groups and leaders. These ideas may be contained in Holy books such as the Bible and the Quran.

CHAPTER 3

WHERE TO FIND INSPIRATIONAL IDEAS?

Synopsis

You can find inspirational ideas from a wide number of sources. In this chapter, we look at some of the places that you can start looking for inspiration.

➢ Where can you find inspirational ideas?

➢ Who can give you inspiration?

You don't have to travel to distant places or go meet famous people to get inspirational ideas. There are many sources of inspiration all around you.

Where To Look

Research

> *"You must be the change that you want to see in the world"*
>
> *Mahatma Gandhi*

There are so many inspirational ideas that you can find by simply conducting research. You may opt to read books or even just research online. You will find a wealth of knowledge from these resources. For instance, there are so many ideas that you can get from Mahatma Gandhi. Since you can't meet this great man in person, you can read his quotes and learn from him.

You can get empowerment by reading quotes from famous people like Mahatma Gandhi. You can find these quote sin different books or online resources.

You can also get inspirational ideas by reading biographies about famous people who managed to succeed no matter what their circumstances may have been. For instance, the biography of the first and only female prime minister of India, Indira Gandhi is a true inspiration. Indira shows what anyone can achieve if they set their mind to it. She was the first woman to ever be elected into office in India. After serving 3 consecutive

30

terms from 1966 to 1977, she was assassinated in 1984 while service her fourth term. This woman shows how determination can enable one achieve what may be termed as the impossible.

Reading Indira Gandhi's story can inspire any person to go beyond their current circumstances and achieve what others may consider to be the impossible.

Search Out New Experiences

If you decide to stay stagnant in life, you will remain exactly that way. You have to open your eyes to new experiences. Sometimes this may mean travelling away from your comfort zones in search of this motivation. For instance, if you live in a small town whereby nobody ever lives or does anything with their lives, you need to venture out of this town. Travelling may inspire you and open your eyes to many possibilities.

You should always seek to find new things and ideas. Don't ever be satisfied with staying at one place for a long time. If you can't travel, you can get imaginative. Read about new places and inspirational stories. Don't just read about people in your own country, try and read about successful people in other parts of the world. This will enlighten you on the opportunities available even outside your own area. You may also find inspiration in nature. Once again, if you can't travel, look for photos and videos. Music may also offer you inspirational ideas. Remember, you need to go out and consider life outside what you are used to. Change may inspire and empower you.

You have to keep an open mind and be ready to embrace change. Sometimes, you will get so many nice inspirational ideas but still have a difficulty in letting them inspire you. This mostly happens when one is reluctant to accept change. This reluctance may come from fear of what lies ahead or even fear of failure. However, you need to allow the inspirational ideas to change your mindset and influence your life. There is no need of having so many great ideas existing only in your mind but not being reflected in your life.

Role Models

These people are full of inspirational ideas that can greatly influence your life. Everyone needs a role model. It doesn't have to be someone famous though. A role model can be someone in your life who encourages and inspires you. It can be a close relative or a friend. Ensure that this person lives the kind of life that you would want to live. Don't just pick any role model. It is also advisable to pick someone who you have something in common with. For instance, people who have been through

32

sexual abuse, tend to look up to Oprah Winfrey and Joyce Meyers as role models. These two women went through that kind of abuse but that didn't limit them in life. They refused to be victims of their past. Their stories can be an inspiration to other girls who have been through the same kind of life.

Meditations

There are many people who believe in the power of meditation. Once you find an inspirational idea, meditating on it can help you commit the idea to your memory. This helps in changing your mindset faster. Yoga also helps with this. There is a lot of inspiration that can be found when you learn to quiet your mind and listen.

Mediating on an inspirational idea can help in changing your mindset. You will accept the idea faster and commit it to memory.

Children

There are so many people who normally get inspired by children. Unlike grownups children lack inhibitions. They also tend to believe in themselves. Their outlook of the world is also innocent. They are still full of dreams that are yet to be crushed by the realities of life. Listening to a child can be a source of inspiration. You can also just watch a child and learn from them.

For instance, see how they select their clothes with so much confidence. If we all learnt to be that confident, we would all be emporewd, We would also learn to trust ourselves and live life to the fullest.

There is so much that can be learnt from a child who trusts her/himself and lacks inhibitions and fears of failure.

Motivational Speakers

You can actually get a wealth of knowledge from motivational speakers. They have so many inspirational ideas that if you listen to can help you change your life. These people have been trained specifically on how to inspire people into living their lives. In addition, they know how to capture a person's attention. They aren't like lecturers who may actually bore you. These speakers know how to keep their topics relevant. You can be very empowered by simply listening to these gurus. Remember, you have to put everything you have learnt into practice so as to get results.

Seminars and Workshops

There are so many seminars and workshops normally held in different areas to inspire people. Sometimes, there may be speakers while other times it's more of a lecture. These meetings are effective in two ways. One can learn a lot and be empowered by the speakers. One can also network with other people and manage to get empowered. Most of the seminars are normally held for people in the same profession or some other type of similarity. This gives enough opportunities for networking and exchanging ideas.

Seminars can be very enlightening. They can help individuals to get inspired and learn new things to empower them.

Inspirational Videos and Tapes

If you can't get to go for a seminar or go listen to a motivational speaker, you can always watch motivational videos. You may find these in your local stores. You can also find a number of them online. Some are free to download while others may cost you some money. These videos can be very beneficial in empowering you to follow your dreams. In addition, they are good since they allow you to watch the replay the videos again and again to keep yourself inspired.

Inspirational People

You can find so many inspirational ideas from inspirational people. These don't have to be the likes of Mahatma Gandhi or Oscar Wilde. You can find just ordinary people living ordinary lives who have managed to overcome some form of adversity. For instance, there are cancer survivors who inspire people. Also, there is a movie called "127 hours" about a man who was trapped in the Grand Canyon for almost a week. To free himself, he had to cut off his arm. These are ordinary people who have managed to inspire people from all over the work. You can get books, videos or even read blogs from such people to get you inspired.

Life Coaching's

There are so many life coaches in today's world. These coaches have written books or made videos. These books contain a wealth of inspirational ideas that can change a person's life. For instance "Simple abundance by Sara...........is a book that has empowered women all over the world. This book normally contains daily readings that help women to learn how to be happy and live a successful life. The simple teachings are very applicable and if used well, they can give good results. There ar4e so many other such books. Some may also be religious. For instance, Bishop T.D Jakes has a number of life coaching books.

There is also inspirational that can be drawn when you try to inspire others. You will also get new ideas that will empower you while you empower other people.

CHAPTER 4

THE PROCESS OF BEING EMPOWERED
THROUGH INSPIRATIONAL IDEAS

Synopsis

There are inspirational ideas everywhere. However, you have to know how to properly use these ideas to empower yourself. In this chapter, we look at how you are supposed to do this.

> How are you supposed to use inspirational ideas?

There are people who have so many ideas yet they don't use them. They read widely and interact with many people yet their live still remain stagnant. There are people who are yet to know how to use the inspiration that they get.

Getting Empowered

What Hinders Empowerment?

There are so many people who go through their lives feeling powerless and uninspired to make anything meaningful out of their lives. Surprisingly, some of these people have all the necessary tools that they need to excel but still have no idea how to use them. In other cases, people may feel powerless due to the circumstances that they are facing. One such circumstance is poverty. Many people feel that they can never be successful because they are poor. They may also be limited due to their inability to access any opportunities because of their financial situations. Poverty also puts one in a situation where it becomes hard to get inspired. For instance, people living in homeless shelters only have their fellow residents to talk to. This brings a general feeling of helplessness since they are all going through the same kind of hardships.

Abuse is another factor that makes many people feels un-empowered and uninspired by life. It robs a person their freedom. It makes them loose their self-esteem and infringe son their privacy. Abuse can ruin a person's life to the point of making them feel hopeless and with no desire to live. Abuse can physical, emotional or even sexual.

A person who feels defeated or helpless may have trouble being empowered. You have to address the root cause of their psychological problems before attempting to inspire them.

Fear of failure is another thing that greatly hinders empowerment. Even with all the right tools and inspired ideas, some people are reluctant to try out new things because of fear.

The Empowerment Process

This process will be different for every single person depending on their circumstances. There are people who may just need to find the right kind of inspiration in order to get started on living their lives. For example, people who lack empowerment due to lack of fear may simply need to overcome this in order to move on. However, abuse takes time.

A person may need counselling and a good support system in order to be empowered. Losing your self-worth is something serious. Trying to re-build may take time. Poverty may also need a different empowerment process. It may have to be eradicated before the process begins. In other cases, one may need to change their mindset in order to overcome the poverty.

In addition, this process will only start after the creation of awareness. There are some people who need to be inspired and empowered. However, they may not even realize this. They are so used to their present situations that they have accepted this as the norm. For such people, they need to be informed about the available opportunities. They have to know that there is more to life than what they are currently experiencing. In addition, they have to realize that they have the ability to achieve everything that they set their mind on.

There should also be efforts put in to help the people get over their frustrations. People who have lacked empowerment throughout their lives generally tend to be very frustrated. To change this mindset takes time. Another feeling that they may be having is anger. They may blame someone else for their current predicament like in cases of. In cases, of abuse; they do have some anger towards their abusers. This will definitely require a lot so as to get over it.

To be empowered, everyone will need a good support system. There are many types of such systems. Some may be financial while others may be emotional. Mentoring can also offer a good support system during the empowerment process. However, all these are vital. However, nobody should ever despair just because they lack someone to support them. With the right inspirational ideas, anyone can be successful. There are so many people who have managed to overcome adversity and leave successful lives even if they had nobody to hold their hands through the whole process.

Participation is a key component of the empowerment process. It's one thing to be full of inspirational ideas and quite a different thing to put these ideas into actions. To be empowered, one must get over the fear of failure and instead take more risks. These risks are the ones that may bear fruits in the long run. If you are trying to empower a group of people, you will have to ensure that they actively participate in the process. They have to overcome their self-confidence issues and try out new activities and ideas.

CHAPTER 5

HOW TO MAKE THE MOST OUT OF INSPIRING IDEAS

Synopsis

Throughout your life, you may come across a number of good inspirational ideas. It is good to know what to do when his happened. In this chapter, we look at how to best use these ideas to be inspired.

 ➤ What can you do in order to make the most out of an inspired idea?

There is a an proverb that says *"Gravesites are the richest places since many who lie there, died with so many great ideas"*. Author unknown

You have to ensure that you make use of all your ideas so as to live a fulfilling life.

How To Do It

Acquiring Inspirational Ideas

The first step is definitely to acquire the ideas. You can do this by going through the processes earlier discussed in chapter. You may also be surprised to find out that you have so many ideas already that you have but have never actually put them into practice. The only way to identify these ideas is by reading widely and interacting with other. For instance, reading this eBook may open your eyes to potential and opportunities that you didn't even realize that you actually possessed.

Write It Down

Oprah Winfrey, one of the world's richest women talked of keeping a notebook by her side at all times of the day or night. In this notebook, she wrote down any inspired thoughts that came to her. She also wrote down all her epiphanies. This is what everyone should have. If you have a nice idea, take a paper and pen and put it down. This will help you in analyzing the idea easily. It will also help you in ensuring that you don't forget the idea or plan. If you have your notebook with you at all times, you will keep referring back to what you wrote down.

You should also have your notebook with you whenever you attend motivational seminars or any other talks that may get you inspired. Even if you are looking for inspiring ideas to empower you from the internet, you have to write everything important. You may listen and get inspired at that time but then forget everything the minute you move on to other activities.

Research

It is always advisable to carry out research on your inspirational ideas before planning on how to put them into action. For instance, if it's a business idea, there is no harm in carrying out further research about the idea before committing your finances into pursuing it. Reading more and consulting with others can inspire you even more. It's never enough to just have a good idea.

Action

You have to put all your inspirational ideas into action. The process of empowerment will only occur once you try out your ideas. For instance, if you are inspired to be a writer, you have to start writing. You can't just keep this idea and keep postponing it for a future date. The time to act is now. Remember, people like Nelson Mandela didn't influence History by just resting on a good idea. They put their ideas into action and were able to get the desired results.

You will only be successful once you put your inspirational ideas into action.

CHAPTER 6

AN OVERVIEW OF LOSING YOUR INSPIRATION

Synopsis

In this chapter, we look at some of the factors that may make someone live an un-inspired life.

> ➢ What makes people lack the motivation to pursue their dreams?

> ➢ How can you avoid being un-inspired?

In life, you can't afford to lose your inspiration. If you do, you may not have much to live for.

If It's Lost

The Power of The Mind

A pessimist will always see the glass as being half empty where as the optimist will see it as being half full. A person's mind greatly influences how they perceive themselves, their dreams and opportunities around them.

Research shows that we all have a lot of power over our mind frames. We can decide to think negatively or positively as befitting our present circumstances. Sometimes we decide to limit our beliefs so as to protect our own egos and self worth. This normally happens especially when failure has occurred in previous circumstances. The self definition of "unlucky" is very powerful mind frames that can greatly affect a person it makes them lack the empowerment that they need to fully live their lives.

A negative mind is something very powerful. Studies show that such minds always keep people living way below their potential. You have to change this. You can do this through positive affirmations and trying to adapt some positivity in your life. Don't just accept every situation in your life. Question and seek to find answers.

Ignorance or Lack Of Knowledge

Lack of knowledge is another reason why people end up living much uninspired lives. For instance, if you are born into a society where girls are not encouraged to pursue further education. You may decide to accept this as the norm. However, if you were enlightened about the true situation, there is no way that you can't accept such a falsehood.

Lack of knowledge may also come from lack of interest to research on things. For instance, if you find have an idea and you don't know much about it. You may decide to fill in the blanks for yourself and discourage yourself from pursuing the idea. You may also end up giving yourself reasons as to why this will never work out for you. Such limiting self-beliefs will make you live much uninspired lives.

To overcome this limitation is not so hard. You just need to educate yourself. You can do this by reading or by being curious enough to find out what others are doing. If you believe that you can't be empowered because you grew up with no finances, you need to read about others who have overcome this inhibition. You can also educate yourself by going through the processes that have been discussed in the third chapter of this eBook.

Negativity

Many people become uninspired due to all the negative voices surrounding them. This voice may be their own or from other people. One may be convinced that they will never amount to much in life. They may also convince themselves that they can't achieve much in life since they may lack something that others may have. This negativity may inhibit one from ever being inspired in life.

Negativity from other people is just as bad if not worse. For instance, a child who grew up with a parent who put them down may have serious self- esteem issues. A teacher who constantly tells his students that they are stupid may make them believe this for the rest of their lives. People who have been in abusive relationships may also go through this kind of negativity. This can make one go through their lives with no confidence and empowerment.

Negativity may also come from friends and family members. They may not have any bad motives but may simply be projecting their fears to you. For instance, a person who may have been disappointed when they failed to realize their dreams may keep warning you about a possibility of going through the same fate. This will give you thoughts of fear of failure which may inhibit your aspirations.

You have to move away from negativity. If there is someone in your life who is hindering your empowerment, you should strive to break free of such a relationship. You should also avoid put yourself down. Try and have a more positive outlook of life. Keep yourself inspired at all times. You can also try and associate with people who have the same ideas that you do. Try and avoid negative people who may discourage you from pursuing your dreams.

Giving up

Getting inspired and empowered takes time and effort. However, some people manage to get this inspiration and get moving. However, they give up if at all they feel that they have not managed to achieve their goals fast enough. You need to learn how to keep trying no matter how much you fail. You can try a different strategy or approach but never give up.

You can a lot from people who have used inspired ideas to make tremendous steps. The Wright brothers didn't manage to make an aeroplane from their first attempt. They kept on failing and their idea actually bore fruits years later. Thomas Edison the man behind the invention of the lamp actually tried a hundred times before he succeeded. You so need to be strong-willed and learn that perseverance is essential.

You can learn how to be perseverant by simply following the below listed tips:

> Never give up even when you feel like you can't possibly make it. You should always remind yourself why you held on for so long in the first place. You can talk to someone who inspired in order to help keep your hopes high.

> You should never lose sight of your ambitions and dreams. Remember in the previous chapter, we mentioned about having a notebook. You should keep referring to this book and look at the plans that you have made. Focusing on your goals will keep you going even when you start feeling hopeless.

> You shouldn't be rigid. Remember, there is a saying that defines madness as the act of repeating the same process over and over again and expecting different results. You should learn how to be flexible. Maybe the

answer to all your problems can simply be found by making minor changes in your approach and strategies.

➢ You need to keep believing in yourself even when nobody else does. It's actually more important to learn how to be confident in yourself than how to get people to be confident in you. You are likely to achieve the later after first achieving the former. You need to believe in your abilities to realize your dreams.

CHAPTER 7

FAMOUS INSPIRATIONAL IDEAS AND PEOPLE THAT HAVE CHANGED THE COURSE OF HISTORY

Synopsis

In this chapter, we get inspired through people who used their inspirational ideas to change the course of History.

> ➤ What is the secret behind being empowered and succeeding in life?

> ➤ Why do others live successful lives while others don't?

One way to get you inspired and motivated is by learning from other empowered people.

Ideas

Leaders

Thomas Jefferson

This is the man behind the initial drafting on the American declaration of independence. This was done on 4th July 1776. There is so much that can be learnt from this great man. First of all, he had a keen interest in reading right from a young age. It is said that he used to study for almost 16 hours each day. This helped him in the acquisition of knowledge and awareness about different things. Remember, in pervious chapters, we emphasized about the cost of ignorance and the importance of getting educated.

We can also learn about persistence from this man. He first ran for presidency in 1776 and lost. He didn't give up though and he managed to take office in the 1800. Through out his life, he tried out a number of ideas which were sometimes rejected by the government and the masses. For instance, he tried to include an act for slavery abolishment in the Declaration. This was however rejected. He also led some campaigns that even led to the arrest of his supporters. However, through sheer determination he managed to realize his dreams and those of millions of Americans.

Martin Luther King Junior

"I have a dream that one day on the hills of Georgia the sons of former slaves and the sons of former slave owners will sit down together at a table of brotherhood".

Martin Luther king Jr

Martin Luther King is remembered as one of America's most vocal civil rights activists. This leader believed in equality of people of all skin colours. This was during a time when racial segregation was very rampant in America. Black people were treated as a minority group and racial discrimination was simply accepted as the norm. He shared his ideas in a non-violent manner that managed to highlight this issue that many had turned a blind eye to. Although he was later assassinated in 1968, Martin Luther King managed to change the courses o History especially for the Black people in America. His inspiration managed to empower millions of people from then up to now. His famous speeches are still an inspiration to many people.

Sir Winston Churchill

This leader is known as one of key figures who shaped Britain's modern history. However, he also played a key role in also the world's history. Churchill played a number of important roles such as politician, author and even soldier. He achieved all this during a time a time when the world was in turmoil and war was going on. He prepared Britain in standing against other world leaders such as Adolf Hitler of Germany. He participated in signing of significant world treaties and boundary agreements.

Winston Churchill also participated in changing the History of other countries such as Kenya in Africa. He managed to end rebellion against the colonial government which was Britain. He also opened up peace talks between the two countries which stayed in place until he lost office.

It is clear to see that a lot can happen simply through one inspired individual. This man used his inspiration to empower many nations across the globe.

Religion Jesus Christ

Jesus Christ is behind the whole Christianity movement. He changed the world and up to now continues to inspire many people who follow his teachings. There is a lot that can be learnt from studying his life. He was the son of a simple carpenter. He was also born in a manager as his parents couldn't find a more suitable place. He led a very simple life. Yet he became a leader to billions of people not just during his time but even now. Many people still turn to him for inspirations. People who have strong faith in him are inspired and empowered to do a lot in life.

Lord Buddha

Lord Buddha is behind the religion of Buddhism. His history differs greatly from Jesus. He had a more privileged birth having been born in a royal family. However, Buddha left prince hood in pursuit of a more noble life. He inspired a lot of people through his teachings on life. It is said that he put himself through meditation and hours and days of fasting and meditations. This man used his inspired ideas and knowledge to inspire people throughout History.

Prophet Muhammad

This Islamic prophet is a pillar of many people of the Islam faith. This prophet went through a lot of hardships in his life having being orphaned at a very early age. He made a living as a shepherd and also a merchant. However, he was not satisfied by the life he was living in Mecca.

This led his to relocating to a cave in the mountains so as to meditate and also have some soul reflections about his life. During this period, He later on got his Revelations from God that he later started preaching to the masses. His views were rejected in Mecca and fearing for his life he had to move to Medina. Although he started out with just a few followers, he later managed to lead very many people. He achieved so much such as ending conflicts in Medina and in other parts of the world.

Science Charles Darwin

This man is simply referred to as the father of evolution. He sorts to study human beings and their origin. He later on came up with scientific proof to show that all human beings have a common origin. Although his thoughts and ideas may have been viewed as being ridiculous at first, they were later accepted by the scientific world in the 1930's.Coming up with his theory wasn't easy. It took years of research and studies. He had to gather enough evidence to prove his theories. This shows what people can achieve through relentless pursuit of their ideas.

Sir Isaac Newton

This is a renowned scientist whose background isn't known by many. Newton was born into a very poor family. His father died while his mother was expectant. Later on he was adopted by his stepfather who he didn't agree with. Although he was a hard working bright student, he had to drop out of school and become a farmer. However, the school headmaster intervened on his behalf and asked his mother to allow him to go back to school. He went to join Cambridge University.

This man is described as one of the world's greatest geniuses. His key area was Mathematics where he came up with many mathematical theories that are being studied in schools up to now. He also made significant contributions to the science world. This includes the development of the telescope, optics and also gravity.

A poor boy went on to become of the world's mathematical and scientific Geniuses. Isaac Newton can inspire anyone to know that they too can achieve a lot in life.

There are many other people, who have used their ideas to make a change in various fields such as, Art and entertainment, heroes and icons and many other areas. Some of these people are famous while others may not be known by many.

CHAPTER 8

HOW TO USE INSPIRATIONAL IDEAS TO EMPOWER OTHERS

Synopsis

This chapter looks at some of the ways in which you can inspire other people.

➤ How can I help others to be empowered?

➤ How can I best share my wisdom and ideas?

Inspiring others can help you stay inspired while at the same time helping in the empowerment of others.

Help Others

Leading by example

You can inspire people by simply living an inspired life. You don't have to flaunt your successes or try to get people to emulate you. People will naturally be inspired by simply observing you. Your successes will make others want to learn from you. Remember people will be inspired by someone who is humble in his pursuits. You also have to be selfless.

Remember, you should never do something just so as to inspire others. You have to find something that you actually enjoy doing. This will also ensure that you are happy whether or not you actually manage to inspire people. You are also more likely to be perseverant if at all you are doing something that you actually enjoy. If not, failure may easily discourage you. You should also be passionate about whatever you are doing. This is another way to ensure that you inspire others.

In leading by example, you also have to learn how to be consistent. Follow the path that you have taken and this will inspire others. However, if you keep jumping from one side to another, people may lose their confidence in you. You can illustrate this through how you act or even the ideas that you share with others.

Learn how to share

If you have the means, then share with as many people as possible. If you can be a motivational speaker, use this try and get good quorums and share your inspirational ideas. There are so many people who get inspired and end up changing their lives just by simply listening to someone.

However, you need a bid platform in order to share your ideas; you can do this even with small groups of people. Talk to people and let them learn from you. If you decide to really do this, commit your time and efforts and ensure that you reach as many people as possible. Keep aiming to reach even bigger groups of people.

You can also get to inspire people by joining a noble cause. This can be another way you can help inspire and empower others. For instance, if you find a cause for helping poor people, you can offer them material support and also impact them morally. Share your ideas with them and inspire them to overcome their present situation. You never know, you may actually end up inspiring people who may one day be detrimental in changing the world.

Mentorship

One way that you can help others to get inspired is through mentorship programs. If you excel in a certain area, you can help others learn the skills to help them excel. For instance, if you are an established writer, you can help other upcoming writers. Share ideas and let them learn from you. This can also be a learning experience for you.

From chapter 8, you will learn that people managed to change History by sharing their ideas with others. They didn't keep them to themselves. Sharing your knowledge may make a big difference in someone else's life as well as yours.

You may have to open up to other people. You don't just have to share your successes. Share your failures and other personal stories that people can relate to. This will not only encourage them but also inspire them. Remember, mentoring isn't just about you. You have to follow the progress of those you are mentoring. Listen to them and work with them.

Be Active

You can't inspire people to do what you have been unable to do. For instance, you can't inspire people to be rich if at all, you have not used your own ideas to be more successful. There is a popular phrase "practice what you preach". People will be more inspired by a person who has managed to be successful in the field that they are attempting to inspire others on. Another example is that you can't inspire artists if at all you aren't one of them. They will doubt your ideas and may not really trust you.

Don't Be Discriminating

You can't be an inspiration to other people if at all you aren't accepting to all. Don't discriminate against people based on gender, race, social status or any other factor that you may not like in them. Learn to listen and talk to people without prejudging them.

To inspire others, learn to accept people from all walks of life.

Don't lose hope

Sometime inspiring people may be very difficult. You may commit your time and effort in an individual only to fail later on. The person may disappoint you or be hesitant in listening to you. However, no matter how discouraged you may be, you have to remain hopeful. Keep trying to be a positive influence on others. With time, you will see the fruits of your labour. Remember, even if you only manage to empower two instead of fifty, this is still a very big accomplishment.

Wrapping up

"Success is the good fortune that comes from aspiration, desperation, perspiration and inspiration".

Evan Esar

There are so many ways that you can recognize a person who is not inspired. One of the ways is in how they think and express themselves. A person who believes that they can't be better than what they are is uninspired. An inspired person always aims to achieve more and become much better at what they are doing. You can also find people who are living way below their potential levels. For instance, you may find a highly educated person stuck in a mediocre career. They may be stuck due to the comfort zone that they have created in this job. They may undersell themselves and even though they know this, they may have no will to change their present circumstances.

One thing that many successful people share is their determination. To be empowered is a process. You have to be willing to embrace change and take risks. You should also be ready to face challenges and still manage to pursue your goals. You have to know what life has to offer you. Find out what your best should be and never settle for less.

Do You Have The Right Mind Frame For Success?

Research shows that we are only able to achieve what we can first perceive in our minds. If you don't believe that you can ever be successful then you are right! Your negative thinking will definitely limit you and end up confirming your self-affirmations. To be a winner, you have to think like one.

There Is No Better Time than Right Now

Have you been thinking about going to school? Opening a business? Venturing into new markets? The time is now. There are so many people who spend their lives making big plans but never follow them through. You have to start living your life right now. Stop making future plans for when you are richer or slimmer or married? If you have an inspired idea, you better put it into action right now.

Don't Give Up No Matter What Happens

You have to be realistic. You may not be able to achieve all your dreams at a go. This may take time and repeat efforts. Take the example of Henry Ford. This multi-billionaire lost his fortune six times without giving up. Now he is accredited to Ford Motors and a lot of other business lines worldwide. He is a success story now. He wouldn't have managed to be one if he had given up due to failure.

Have confident and believe in your ability to achieve your goals. If you believe that you can do it then you definitely can.

The future offers a lot of possibilities for you. You can decide to get inspired and change the course of your life.

Remember, every new day is another opportunity for you to realize your dreams. Dawn signifies a new fresh start and As long as you are alive, you have to keep on trying.

Good Luck!

Printed by Libri Plureos GmbH in Hamburg,
Germany